MORNING POEMS

Also by Robert Bly

Meditations on the Insatiable Soul
What Have I Ever Lost by Dying?
Selected Poems
The Light Around the Body
The Rag and Bone Shop of the Heart
American Poetry
Iron John
The Sibling Society

MORNING POEMS

Robert Bly

HarperFlamingo
An Imprint of HarperCollins*Publishers*

I am grateful to the editors of the following magazines, in whose pages some of these poems first appeared: *Agni, American Poetry Review, The Atlantic Monthly, Beloit Poetry Journal, Bennington Review, Black Moon, Blind Donkey, Boulevard, Chrysalis, The Chicago Review, Columbia Review, Common Boundary, The Gettysburg Review, Harvard Review, The Hudson Review, Image: A Journal of the Arts and Religion, Kestrel, The Lower Stumpf Lake Review, Manhattan Review, The Nation, The New Republic, The Northern Reader, The North Stone Review, Pequod, The Plum Review, Poetry Ireland Review, Salmagundi, Sphinx, The Sun, West Hills Review, The William and Mary Review, Witness,* and *The Yale Review.*

"Waking on the Farm," "He Wanted to Live His Life Over," "The Bear and the Man," and "A Farm in Western Minnesota" were first published in *Poetry.*

Part 3 of "It's As If Someone Else Is with Me" originally appeared as "The Beehive" in *Contemporary American Poetry,* edited by A. Poulin, Jr.

"Wallace Stevens and Mozart" originally appeared as "Wallace Stevens and Florence" in *Meditations on the Insatiable Soul,* HarperCollins Publishers, 1994, and "Rethinking Wallace Stevens" first appeared as "Words with Wallace Stevens" in *Gratitude for Old Teachers,* BOA Editions, Ltd., 1993.

A hardcover edition of this book was published in 1997 by
HarperCollins Publishers.

HarperCollins books may be purchased for educational, business, or sales promotional use. For information please write: Special Markets Department, HarperCollins Publishers, Inc., 10 East 53rd Street, New York, NY 10022.

First HarperFlamingo edition published 1998.

Designed by Joseph Rutt

The Library of Congress has catalogued the hardcover edition as follows:

Bly, Robert.
Morning poems / Robert Bly.
p. cm.
ISBN 0-06-018251-2
I. Title.
PS3552.L9M63   1997
811'.54—dc21   97-1502

ISBN 0-06-092873-5 (pbk.)

98 99 00 01 02 ❖/RRD 10 9 8 7 6 5 4 3 2 1

For Ruth

CONTENTS

I

II

I

Early Morning in Your Room

It's morning. The brown scoops of coffee, the
   wasplike
Coffee grinder, the neighbors still asleep.
The gray light as you pour gleaming water—
It seems you've travelled years to get here.

Finally you deserve a house. If not deserve
It, have it; no one can get you out. Misery
Had its way, poverty, no money at least;
Or maybe it was confusion. But that's over.

Now you have a room. Those light-hearted books:
The Anatomy of Melancholy, Kafka's *Letter
To His Father*, are all here. You can dance
With only one leg, and see the snowflake falling

With only one eye. Even the blind man
Can see. That's what they say. If you had
A sad childhood, so what? When Robert Burton
Said he was melancholy, he meant he was home.

The Shocks We Put Our Pitchforks Into

The shocks said that winter
Was coming. Each stood there,
Said, "I've given myself away.
Take me. It's over."

And we did. With the shiny tips
Of our forks, their handles so
Healthy and elegant,
We slipped each bundle free,

Gave it to the load.
Each bundle was like
A soul, tucked back
Into the cloud of souls.

That's how it will be
After death—such an abundance
Of souls, all together—
None tired, in the heavy wagon.

Why We Don't Die

In late September many voices
Tell you you will die.
That leaf says it. That coolness.
All of them are right.

Our many souls—what
Can they do about it?
Nothing. They're already
Part of the invisible.

Our souls have been
Longing to go home
Anyway. "It's late," they say.
"Lock the door, let's go."

The body doesn't agree. It says,
"We buried a little iron
Ball under that tree.
Let's go get it."

HAWTHORNE AND THE ELEPHANT

Hawthorne's walking stick—very short—lay
Under glass at the Customs House. On the wharf,
A crab shell, emptied by a gull, lies alone.
His walking sticks lie near . . . but the crab is gone,
Like Hawthorne. Bedrooms were low;
You were taxed for high ceilings in those days.
Ships brought licorice and peppers. Hawthorne's
 father
Died of a fever off the coast of Sumatra,
Guides say, and *America*, his ship, brought
The first elephant here in 1794.
Water got short on the way; to save the elephant
They gave her thirty bottles of beer a day.
She—Bette—died in Maine, an alcoholic.
How alert we were at the House of Seven Gables!
Clifford's room is the little one up the secret stairs.

THE OLD WOMAN FRYING PERCH

Have you heard about the boy who walked by
The black water? I won't say much more.
Let's wait a few years. It wanted to be entered.
Sometimes a man walks by a pond, and a hand
Reaches out and pulls him in.
                              There was no
Malice, exactly. The pond was lonely, or needed
Calcium. Bones would do. What happened then?

It was a little like the night wind, which is soft,
And moves slowly, sighing like an old woman
In her kitchen late at night, moving pans
About, lighting a fire, frying some perch for the cat.

For Donald Hall

Conversation with the Soul

The soul said, "Give me something to look at."
So I gave her a farm. She said,
"It's too large." So I gave her a field.
The two of us sat down.

Sometimes I would fall in love with a lake
Or a pine cone. But I liked her
Most. She knew it.
"Keep writing," she said.

So I did. Each time the new snow fell,
We would be married again.
The holy dead sat down by our bed.
This went on for years.

"This field is getting too small," she said.
"Don't you know anyone else
To fall in love with?"
What would you have said to Her?

He Wanted to Live His Life Over

What? You want to live your life over again?
"Well, I suppose, yes . . . That time in Grand Rapids . . .
My life—as I lived it—was a series of shynesses."

Being bolder—what good would that do?
"I'd open my door again. I've felt abashed,
You see. Now I'd go out and say, 'All right,

I'll go with you to Alaska.' Just opening the door
From inside would have altered me—a little.
I'm too shy . . ." *And so, a bolder life*

Is what you want? "We could begin now.
Just walk with me—down to the river.
I'll pretend this boat is my life . . . I'll climb in."

9

The Glimpse of Something in the Oven

Childhood is like a kitchen. It is dangerous
To the mice, but the husband gets fed; he's
An old giant, grumbling and smelling children.
The kitchen is a place where you get smaller

And smaller, or you lose track. In general
You become preoccupied with this old lady
In the kitchen. . . . She putters about, opens oven
    doors.
The thing is the old woman won't *discuss* anything.

The giant will. He's always been a fan of Aristotle,
Knew him at school. It is no surprise to him
That the Trojan War lasted ten years, or how it
Ended. He knows something you don't.

Your sister says, "Say, what's that in the oven?"

Bad People

A man told me once that all the bad people
Were needed. Maybe not all, but your fingernails
You need; they are really claws, and we know
Claws. The sharks—what about them?
They make other fish swim faster. The hard-faced
   men
In black coats who chase you for hours
In dreams—that's the only way to get you
To the shore. Sometimes those hard women
Who abandon you get you to say, "You."
A lazy part of us is like a tumbleweed.
It doesn't move on its own. Sometimes it takes
A lot of Depression to get tumbleweeds moving.
Then they blow across three or four States.
This man told me that things work together.
Bad handwriting sometimes leads to new ideas;
And a careless god—who refuses to let people
Eat from the Tree of Knowledge—can lead
To books, and eventually to us. We write
Poems with lies in them, but they help a little.

Things to Think

Think in ways you've never thought before.
If the phone rings, think of it as carrying a message
Larger than anything you've ever heard,
Vaster than a hundred lines of Yeats.

Think that someone may bring a bear to your door,
Maybe wounded and deranged; or think that a moose
Has risen out of the lake, and he's carrying on his
    antlers
A child of your own whom you've never seen.

When someone knocks on the door, think that he's
    about
To give you something large: tell you you're
    forgiven,
Or that it's not necessary to work all the time, or that
    it's
Been decided that if you lie down no one will die.

Two Ways to Write Poems

"I am who I am." I wonder what one has to pay
To say that. I couldn't do it. For years
I thought, "You are who you are." But maybe
You weren't. Maybe you were someone else.

Sam's friend, who loved poetry, played football
In school even though he didn't want to.
He got hit. Later he said to me, "I write poems.
I am who I am . . . but my neck hurts."

How many times I have begun a poem
Before I knew what the main sounds
Would be. We find out. Toward the end
The poem is just beginning to be who it is.

That's all right, but there's another way as well.
One picks the rhyme words, and so the main
Sounds, before one begins. I wonder what
Yeats had to pay in order to do that.

The Barn at Elabuga

What is it like to "get killed"? Getting killed
Happens during a war a lot to horses and people.
This time there's no long struggle in the bedroom,
No hoarse cries and confessions after which the clock
Stops, and the priest needs some coffee in the kitchen.
Just being killed leaves you small and unattached.
The boy aiming the mortar makes a mistake
And horses crazed by the noise kill your father
While he is feeding geese. Those times our family
Died that way haven't left any mark on us.
But I could ask why my thumb keeps moving
Around my forefinger when I read, or why that line
Comes down from my mouth. We do know that
    people
At the end of a war tend to hang themselves
In the nearest barn, without telling anyone.

THE RUSSIAN

"The Russians had few doctors on the front line.
My father's job was this: after the battle
Was over, he'd walk among the men hit,
Sit down and ask: 'Would you like to die on your
Own in a few hours, or should I finish it?'
Most said, 'Don't leave me.' The two would have
A cigarette. He'd take out his small notebook—
We had no dogtags, you know—and write the man's
Name down, his wife's, his children, his address, and
    what
He wanted to say. When the cigarette was done,
The soldier would turn his head to the side. My
    father
Finished off four hundred men that way during the
    war.
He never went crazy. They were his people.

He came to Toronto. My father in the summers
Would stand on the lawn with a hose, watering
The grass that way. It took a long time. He'd talk
To the moon, to the wind. 'I can hear you growing'—
He'd say to the grass. 'We come and go.
We're no different from each other. We are all

Part of something. We have a home.' When I was
   thirteen,
I said, 'Dad, do you know they've invented sprinklers
Now?' He went on watering the grass.
'This is my life. Just shut up if you don't understand
   it.'"

II

Some Men Find It Hard to Finish Sentences

Sometimes a man can't say
What he . . . A wind comes
And his doors don't rattle. Rain
Comes and his hair is dry.

"There's a lot to keep inside
And a lot to . . ." "Sometimes shame
Means we . . ." Children are cruel.
"He's six and his hands . . ."

Even Hamlet kept passing
The King praying
And the King said,
"There was something . . ."

VISITING THE EIGHTY-FIVE-YEAR-OLD POET

The eighty-five-year-old man stands up,
And walks to the bookcase, his hair tousled,
His legs thin, to fetch a book, then pulls
It down and says, "No doubt you've already read
    this?"

He has. He paddles among these ice floes,
These enormous fat books, like a great Eskimo
Hunter, for there are seals below in the sea,
Offering their hides, their fat, their great lonesome
    eyes.

"*Oh* yes!" he says, "*Oh* yes." Some truths have been
Said. Someone in China or Hardanger has written
    great
Poems. "*Oh* yes." He stands again, goes to the wall.
"Emerson was a *keen* reader. *Oh* yes!"

He has lived his whole life on three acres
Of apple trees, chopping wood, visiting
The madhouse, throwing plates against the wall,
Translating, packing apples, writing poems.

I am proud to know him, this old man late in life
Who stands up and says, "No doubt you've already
    lived this?"

For the Norwegian poet Olav H. Hauge

ALL THESE STORIES

There are so many stories. In one, a bear
Marries a sailing ship, and they have children
Who are islands (covered with low brush).
In another an obstinate woman floats upstream.

Or the child wailing on a rock, set ashore
By her seal mother (her real mother), waits
And wails, and faces appear at windows until
Charlotte Brontë agrees to begin her novel.

You know stories like that. The Terrible Nurse
Throws the Daughter into the sea. A whale
Swallows her, and she is free from husband
And children long enough to be herself.

Something in us wants things to happen.
We twist our ankle and end up reading Gibbon.
In some dreams a wolf pursues us until we
Turn into swallows, and agree to live in longing.

THE RESEMBLANCE BETWEEN
YOUR LIFE AND A DOG

I never intended to have this life, believe me—
It just happened. You know how dogs turn up
At a farm, and they wag but can't explain.

It's good if you can accept your life—you'll notice
Your face has become deranged trying to adjust
To it. Your face thought your life would look

Like your bedroom mirror when you were ten.
That was a clear river touched by mountain wind.
Even your parents can't believe how much you've
        changed.

Sparrows in winter, if you've ever held one, all
        feathers,
Burst out of your hand with a fiery glee.
You see them later in hedges. Teachers praise you,

But you can't quite get back to the winter sparrow.
Your life is a dog. He's been hungry for miles,
Doesn't particularly like you, but gives up, and
        comes in.

Reading in a Boat

I was glad to be in that boat, floating
Under oak leaves that had been
Carved by crafty light.

How many times during the night
I laughed, because She
Came near, and stayed, or returned.

The boat stopped, and I woke.
But the pages kept turning. I jumped
Back in the book, and caught up.

I was not in pain, not hungry,
Friend, I was alive, sleeping,
And all that time reading a book.

Waking on the Farm

I can remember the early mornings—how the
    stubble,
A little proud with frost, snapped as we walked.

How the John Deere tractor hood pulled heat
Away from our hands when we filled it up with gas.

And the way the sun brought light right out of the
    ground.
It turned on a whole hill of stubble as easily as a
    single stone.

Breathing seemed frail and daring in the morning.
To pull in air was like reading a whole novel.

The angleworms, turned up by the plow, looked
Uneasy, like shy people trying to avoid praise.

For a while we had goats. They were like turkeys
Only more reckless. One butted a red Chevrolet.

When we washed up at noon, we were more
    ordinary.
But the water kept something in it of the early
    morning.

When Threshing Time Ends

There is a time. Things end.
The fields are clean.
Belts are put away.
And the horses go home.

What is left endures
In the minds of boys
Who wanted this joy
Never to end.

The splashing of hands,
Jokes and oats:
It was a music
Touching and fervent.

The Bible was right.
Presences come and go.
Wash in cold water.
The fire has moved.

A Family Photograph, Sunday Morning, 1940

They've gathered on the farm lawn, ten people, all
   ages.
Esther Berg's hair has waves like Clara Bow's;
The women look as if they have too much to do.
One boy smiles—it is me—and looks down. He
   seems glad,
But his sweater sleeve is too short. The men's hands,
None placed in pockets, all hang down.
They look as if they wanted to grasp something.
The men smile, but their eyes say hard things.
"The world pulls at me—it tore my father
Away already. That forty-acre farm he bought
By Marietta is still black. I have to go now."
It was nineteen-forty, grasshoppers, hard times.
Two old women who guard the group on both sides
Take nothing on trust. "I trust my hands, and that's
   all."

A Farm in Western Minnesota

When I look at childhood, I see the yellow rosebush
Grandma planted near her door, the gravel
Beneath the bicycle tires, and the new legs pumping
As we raced along; and the roads that invited us
West—only a mile from home the land began to rise.

We tried those wind chargers. My father
Was open to any new idea, and one day
A thousand sheep—starving—arrived in cattle cars
From Montana—almost free. We took four
Hundred. How thin they were! Some lived for years.

Many rooms were cold at night, and the hired men
Didn't have much of a life. Sometimes they'd just
    leave.
I remember my father throwing dead ewes over
The edge of the gravel pit. It was efficient. There
Was work to do, but no one learned how to say
    goodbye.

For a Childhood Friend, Marie

She knew a lot about life on a farm: wagon
Poles that sometimes broke, and grown men
Pinned against the fencepost by a bull.
Sometimes you tie a favorite lamb
To a tree so that the old bucks will not kill him,
And he hangs himself from the rope.
Movies Saturday night—girls laughed
Behind their sleeves, at men or boys.
Marie, thirty years old, still loved
The high school, the tall boys, gossip
About the teachers, the proms. She also
Loved our lives that were not going
So well. She married the hired man—
My grandmother told her not to—and he drank.

What the Animals Paid

The Hampshire ewes standing in their wooden pens,
Their shiny black hooves close to each other,

Had to pay with their wool, with their wombs,
With their eating, with their fear of the dogs.

Every animal had to pay. Horses paid all day;
They pulled stone-boats and the ground pulled back.

And the pigs? They paid with their squealing
When the knife entered the throat and the blood

Followed it out. The blood, steaming and personal,
Paid it. Any debt left over the intestines paid.

"I am what I am." The pig could not say that.
The women paid with their bowed heads, and the
     men,

My father among them, paid with their drinking.
Demons shouted: "Pay to the last drop!" I paid

The debt another way. Because I did not pay
In the farm way, I am writing this poem today.

The Bear and the Man

Suppose there were a bear and a man. The bear
Knows his kin—old pebbles, fifty-five-
Gallon barrels, big pine trees in the moonlight,
Abandoned down jackets; and the man approaches
    warily—

He's read Tolstoy, knows a few symphonies.
That's about it. Each has lost a son. The bear's
Killed by a trap, the man's killed by a bear.
That boy was partly drunk, alone in the woods.

The bear puts out black claws firmly on earth.
He's not dumb. Skinned, he's like a man. People
Say that both bears and men receive a signal
Coming from far up there, near the North Pole.

When My Dead Father Called

Last night I dreamt my father called to us.
He was stuck somewhere. It took us
A long time to dress, I don't know why.
The night was snowy; there were long black roads.

Finally, we reached the little town, Bellingham.
There he stood, by a streetlamp in cold wind,
Snow blowing along the sidewalk. I noticed
The uneven sort of shoes that men wore

In the early Forties. And overalls. He was smoking.
Why did it take us so long to get going? Perhaps
He left us somewhere once, or did I simply
Forget he was alone in winter in some town?

III

THE GREEN COOKSTOVE

A lonely man once sat on a large flat stone.
When he lifted it, he saw a kitchen: a green
Enamel range with big claw feet, familiar.
Someone lives in that room, cooking and cackling.

"I saw her once," Virgil said. "She was Helen's
Younger sister." Helen's betrayed husband
Sits by the window, peeling garlic cloves,
And throwing crusts to Plymouth Rocks.

We'll never understand this. Somewhere below
The flat stone of the skull, a carnivorous couple
Lives and plans future wars. Are we innocent?
These wars don't happen by accident—they occur

Too regularly. How often do we lift the plate
At the bottom of our brain and throw some garlic
And grain down to the kitchen? "Keep cooking,
My dears," we say. "Something good will come of
    this."

The Playful Deeds of the Wind

Sometimes there's the wind. Sometimes the wind
Takes a certain scrap of paper, and blows
It back into the Bible. Then your family line
Is whole, and your great-great-grandparents
Stretch out in the coffin, and rest. That's something
Wind can do. Sometimes wind blows
A skirt up an inch or two, and the body
Signs a contract for its novel; then babies
Come, and people sit at breakfast, and the old
Words get spoken. Or the wind blows an ash
Into the anarchist's eye, and he pulls
The trigger too soon, and kills the King instead of
The fat factory owner, and then
A lot of men get on motorcycles. They
Dig trenches, and the wind blows the gas
Here and there, and you and I get nothing
Out of that wind except blind uncles
And a boy at the table who can't say "Please."

It Is So Easy to Give In

I have been thinking about the man who gives in.
Have you heard about him? In this story
A twenty-eight-foot pine meets a small wind
And the pine bends all the way over to the ground.

"I was persuaded," the pine says. "It was
    convincing."
A mouse visits a cat, and the cat agrees
To drown all her children. "What could I do?"
The cat said. "The mouse *needed* that."

It's strange. I've heard that some people conspire
In their own ruin. A fool says, "You don't
Deserve to live." The man says, "I'll string this rope
Over that branch, maybe you can find a box."

The Great One with her necklace of skulls says,
"I need twenty thousand corpses." "Tell you what,"
The General says, "we have an extra battalion
Over there on the hill. We don't need all these men."

WANTING MORE APPLAUSE
AT A CONFERENCE

It's something about envy. I won't say I'm envious,
But I did have certain moods when I was two.
Now of course I can't remember any of that.
I'm happy if another receives some attention

That's really mine. I talk, and the man next to me
Talks, and he gets the applause. Or I am confused
And she makes sense. This is hard to bear.
I bear it, but it causes trouble inside the den.

Is it a mammal problem then? Six teats are palpable
Far inside the wiry fur, and I want more
Than one? Is that it? It is, but such greed
Is mainly a problem for small mammals,

And I am no longer small. Let's call it a mood
When we can't remember. Let's call it a habit
Of opening the mouth when we, who have
Much, want more, even what belongs to the poor.

Making Smoke

There was a boy who never got enough.
It's not unusual. Something
In him longed to find the big
Mother, and he leaped into the sea.

It took a while, but a whale
Agreed to swallow him.
He knew it was wrong, but once
Past the baleen, it was too late.

It's OK. There's a curved library
Inside, and those high
Ladders. People take requests.
It's like the British Museum.

One needs a fire to get out.
Maybe it was the romance
Novels he burned. Smoke curls
Up the whale's gorge. She coughs,

And that's it. He swims to shore;
It's a fishing town in Alaska.
He calls his father. "I'm here.
Let me tell you a story."

Thinking About Old Jobs

Well, let's say this morning is all of life there is—
Let's suppose the weather (rainy), the room
(Creamy-walled), the bed (soft), your cells (calm,
Excitable, and dense) are it. Don't expect more.

Then what? Does it matter how you chose
To live at twenty? You felt detached, let's say,
So you blew your legs and arms off.
Why feel bad? It helped in some ways.

You had more solitude, because friends avoid stumps.
Of course you had to live. You started picking
Other people's cucumbers with your teeth,
As you lay flat on a board. Don't be ashamed.

It was a deal. It worked. The boss's children
Later sent you back the cancelled contract.
Then remember the job you had lying about
Your health to life insurance companies?

Or performing as a Santa in Depression wards?
All those jobs were all right. But that time is over.
Am I content? I am. But we don't
Have to live in the way we did then: Let's talk.

Conversation with a Monster

A man I knew could never say who he was.
You know people like that. When he met a monster,
He'd encourage the monster to talk about eating
But failed to say that he objected to being prey.

A day goes by; a week; a month; it's summer.
The adolescent wolverines go out scouting;
Crabs lift their claws; the praying mantis
Get religious. This man keeps trying to adapt.

Adopt? Be adopted? It's funny, but those born
From eggs seem not to feel homeless. Something
Pushes them out, and they fly to sea, or swim
Up from the gravel, milkily transparent, and they're
    gone.

This man went up to monsters and asked to be
Adopted. I've done that often. Reader, are you
Fond of the Jonah story? Say to a monster,
"I may have something for you, but I can't promise."

The Black Figure Below the Boat

We hear phrases: "He made me do it."
"I never wanted that." The boy's boat gets
Pushed out on the sea, and before long the tidal
Currents guide it from beneath. He goes to sleep.

He meets a woman, and marries her even though
He doesn't want to. He says, "It was the current."
But some tiny black figure swims below the boat,
Pushing it. This man or god works all night.

Then what? Months go by, years, twenty years.
A lot of water. The boat hits gravel.
It's an island—the kind where giants live.
"Don't say you didn't want it. Just get ready."

THE MAN WHO DIDN'T KNOW WHAT WAS HIS

There was a man who didn't know what was his.
He thought as a boy that some demon forced him
To wear "his" clothes and live in "his" room
And sit on "his" chair and be a child of "his" parents.

Each time he sat down to dinner, it happened again.
His own birthday party belonged to someone else.
And—was it sweet potatoes that he liked?—
He should resist them. Whose plate is this?

This man will be like a lean-to attached
To a house. It doesn't *have* a foundation.
This man is helpful and hostile in each moment.
This man leans toward you and leans away.

He's charming, this man who doesn't know what is
    his.

The Mouse

It's good to have poems
That begin with tea,
And end with God.

A man is drinking tea,
Let's say, and a mouse
Runs across the floor.

It makes him think
Of all hidden things.
A mouse is a furry

Cruelty with paws.
It's a secret with ears,
A shame the man

Thought he could tell
No one of, a shame
That searches quietly

For kernels of grain
Below that awful
Cat of Augustine.

The Storm

A sadness comes when we think back.
The car says, "I will bring you home."
Confusion says, "Is it all clear?"
The driver says, "A storm is coming."

The car was still warming up
When the storm came. Like all storms,
It lacked subtlety and obeyed
Something or someone irresistible.

The people stood looking out at the car.
There wasn't room for everyone.
Someone would be left behind
In the cold house. Human longing

Says, "I know there's a better place."
The car says, "Let's stop talking and go."
Confusion says that we're quite clear about it.
And the storm says, "Here I come."

The Yellow Dot

God does what she wants. She has very large
Tractors. She lives at night in the sewing room
Doing stitchery. Then chunks of land at mid-
Sea disappear. The husband knows that his wife
Is still breathing. God has arranged the open
Grave. That grave is not what we want,
But to God it's a tiny hole, and he has
The needle, draws thread through it, and soon
A nice pattern appears. The husband cries,
"Don't let her die!" But God says, "I
Need a yellow dot here, near the mailbox."

The husband is angry. But the turbulent ocean
Is like a chicken scratching for seeds. It doesn't
Mean anything, and the chicken's claws will tear
A Rembrandt drawing if you put it down.

In memory of Jane Kenyon

IV

It's As If Someone Else Is with Me

I.

It's as if someone else is here with me, here in this
   room
In which I lie. The longing the ear feels for sound
Has given me the sweetness that I confuse with Her.

The joy of being alone, eating the honey of words.
The white-walled room, and Stevens, and the sun.
This is the joy of the soul that has preserved
Itself despite fleas and soap in the light-hearted sun.

One is not alone when one is alone, if She
Is here. It is a She that no one loves, a She
That one loves when one loves what one does love.

2.

November is gone, bare trees, winter.
At nightfall the lonely streets fill with
Ice and cars. Loneliness fills my chest,
As if I walked all night by the North Sea.

I am here, somewhere near the edge of life,
A warm room, lamps, some poems I love—
To nudge a poem along toward its beauty—
Is that selfishness? Is it something silly?

Do others love doing this? Longing
To find her in a phrase, and be close
There, kissing the walls and the doorframe.
Happy in the change of a single word.

3.

A lamp pours light into the room, and it's your
Room, and you write poems there. You never
Tire of the curving lines, and the freedom of the
    sounds,
And the demons peering around the molding.

The beauty that six or seven words can bring
Together makes the whole brain sing.
And I feel like a single-souled cook in the Middle
Ages praising God in the kitchen pans.

But our praise is more like humming of bees.
What if a beehive were run this way? Who would
Eat up all the honey? Don't worry about it.
The workers say, "I'll fly out and be religious."

4.

It's morning and it's calm. And the man
Writes along, inviting this detail
And that—looking toward some playful life.
What life? Oh never mind—the life of language.

And thinking. Longing waves one arm,
And the woman inside us looks out
From her eternal indolences, feeding
The hummingbirds with her flowery thoughts.

I lie here with a cover and coffee and a pen,
Feeling delight in being a child of language—
Neither man nor woman exactly, but a young monk
In a skin boat, bobbing among the seals of sound.

5.

I've been thinking about these little adventures
In morning longing—these embarkations,
Excursions in round hide-boats on the sea,
Passing over the beings far below.

The deep vowels—perhaps whales—mourn
And sing at their stone table five miles down
On the ocean floor. They mourn some loss.
But the small finny sounds, the *ers* and *ins*

And *ors* and *ings,* mourn as well—we don't
Know what. Perhaps vowels were all created
In a moment of sorrow before creation—
A grief they've not been able to sing in this life.

6.

It's good to stay in bed a while, and hear
The *ay* slyly hidden in sequacious,
Scent in summer world the two *ers,*
Listen for the *in* hidden in woodbins.

Am I like the hog snuffling for truffles,
Followed by skimpy lords in oversized furs?
For this gaiety do I need forgiveness?
Does the lark need forgiveness for its blue eggs?

So it's a bird-like thing then, this hiding
And warming of sounds. They are the little low
Heavens in the nest; now my chest feathers
Widen, now I'm an old hen, now I am satisfied.

7.

The world is its usual rich self. Disturbed news
Came before sleep, then hours below light, finally
A return to coffee and the joy of unfinished poems.
It is early October, bright leaves falling everywhere.

What could it mean that such sharp leaves fall?
Does it imply that the best are called first?
Do we long to think that when a baby
Dies early it nevertheless blesses the stars?

I don't want to imply such abundance of meaning
Exists in me. A lamppost shines over
The ocean. The waves take what they want of the
    light.
The rest they give back, to the hospitals and the poor.

8.

The dawn comes. Leaves feel it's time
To say something, and I feel myself drawn
To You. I know this is wrong.

To be drawn to You can cause trouble;
I do so against all advice, from that one
In me who saved me by keeping me alone.

I've lived in so many houses, where
You were not. If You became a dock
I became a boat and pushed away.

Those who are drawn to You become land
If You are land, or water if You are water.
I want nothing from You but to see You.

A WEEK OF POEMS AT BENNINGTON

THE DOG'S EARS

A little snow. Coffee. The bowled-over branches,
The wind; it is cold outdoors; but in the bed
It's warm, in the early lamp-light, reading poems.

These fingers, so rosy, so alive, move about
This book. Here is my wide-travelling palm,
The thumb that looks like my father's, the wedding
    ring.

It's time to prepare myself, as a friend suggested,
"Not to be here." It will happen. People will say,
"That day the dish lay empty on the brown table.

"The gold knob shone alone in the dark.
The light came in, and no eyes received it,
And bits of ice hung on the dog's ears."

WHEN THE CAT STOLE THE MILK

Well there it is. There's nothing to do.
The cat steals the milk and it's gone.
Then the cat steals you, and you're found
Days later, with milk on your face.

That implies that you become whoever
Steals you. The trees steal a man,
And an old birch becomes his wife
And they live together in the woods.

Some of us have always wanted
God to steal us. Then our friends
Would call each other, and print
Posters, and we would never be found.

Being Happy All Night

It's as if the mice stayed warm inside the snow,
As if my cells heard laughing from the Roman
    vineyards.
Mice slept despite the cruel songs of the stars.
We laughed and woke and sniffed and slept again.

Some people inside my body last night
Married each other just in order to dance.
And Sara Grethe smiled so proudly the men
Kicked their heels on the planks, but kept the beat.

Oh I think it was the books I read long ago.
It's as if I joined other readers on a long road.
We found dead men hanging in a meadow.
We took dew from the grass and washed our eyes.

For S.B.

THE WIDOWED FRIEND

I hear rustlings from the next room; and he is ready
To leave. "See you tomorrow." A long line
Of feeling follows him out the door. He carries
On his shoulders—which slope a little—a divorce,

Prosody, marital love as pertinacious
As a bulldog's mouth, a grandfather, grand-
Mother. Land and death weigh him down, so he
Becomes a large man on a thin bridge walking.

If, now, he lives alone, who will hear
The thin cough in the morning, who will hear
The milk hitting the pail when the old man sings?
Who will notice the forty drafts on yellow paper?

It's up to us to see him, call him, and say,
"Stay, friend, be with us, tell me what happened."

For D.H.

We Only Say That

"There are so many things to love around here."
We only say that when we want to hint
Something—the day after we notice a woman,
Who waves a hand with her female bravery.

We say, "The icicles are really brilliant today!"
Or, "Let's make fun of other people."
That would bring us closer. Or "Martha brought
Her dog out into the morning snow."

Her hand reaches up to brush her neck,
Or she puts on her boots. A voice inside us
Says, "Oh a woman! Let's close the door.
Let's flirt and not flirt. Let's play cards and laugh."

WOUNDING OTHERS

Well I do it, and it's done.
And it can't be taken back.
There's a wound in my chest
Where I wounded others.

But it will knit, or heal, in time.
That's what you say.
And some that I wounded
Claim: "I am the better for it."

Was it truth-telling or
A thin man with a knife?
The wound will close, or heal
In time. That's what you say.

WHAT THE BUTTOCKS THINK

Don't tell me that nothing can be done.
The tongue says, "I know I can change things."
The toe says, "I have my ways."
The heart is weeping and remembering Eden.

Legs think that a good run will do it.
Tongue has free tickets; he'll fly to heaven.
But the buttocks see everything upside down:
They want you to put your head down there,

Remind the heart it was upside down
In the womb, so that when your mother,
Knowing exactly where she was going,
Walked upstairs, you weren't going anywhere.

What Bill Stafford Was Like

With small steps he climbed very high mountains
And offered distinctions to persuasive storms,
Delicacies at the edge of something larger,
A comfort in walking on ground close to water.

Something large, but it wasn't an animal snorting
In a cave, more like the rustling of a thousand
Small-winged birds, all together, comfortable,
In a field, feeding. One felt at home nearby.

There are many possible ways to see the world
(To whom we should be fair). When someone
Spoke, his face thought, and his eyebrow
Said it. The words weren't always comforting,

But calculated to nudge us along to that place
—Just over there—where we would be safe for the
    night.

A Poem Is Some Remembering

It's morning; there's lamplight, and the room is still.
All night as we slept, memory flowed
Onto the brain shore. Memories rise and fall
And leave behind a delicate openness to death.

Almost a longing to die. That longing
Is like rain on canyon ground, only droplets.
And the brain is like brown sand, it stretches
On and on, and it absorbs the rain.

What is a poem? "Oh it is some remembering,"
A woman said to me. "Thousands of years ago,
When I stood by a grave, a woman handed
Me a small bone made red with ochre.

"It was a poem about heaven, and I wept so."

WALLACE STEVENS AND MOZART

Oh Wallace Stevens, dear friend,
You are such a pest. You are so sure.
You think everyone is in *your* family.

It is you and your father and Mozart,
And ladies tasting cold rain in Florence,
Puzzling out inscriptions, studying the gold flake.

It is as if life were a visit to Florence,
A place where there are no maggots in the flesh,
No one screaming, no one afraid.

Your job, your joy, your morning walk,
As if you walked on the wire of the mind,
High above the elephants; you cry out a little but
    never fall.

As if we could walk always high above the world,
No bears, no witches, no Macbeth,
No one screaming, no one in pain, no one afraid.

RETHINKING WALLACE STEVENS

What can I say? You have this funny
Idea that the gods are dead.

You were so rash. I'd *play* saying
The gods have died, but I'd never *say* it.

If they're gone, only Imagination
Can replace them. That's you.

We'll have to come to you, where
You stand in your Hartford garden,

Looking and lolling and longing
Like a girl in a white dress.

Tasting Heaven

Some people say that every poem should have
God in it somewhere. But of course Wallace Stevens
Wasn't one of those. We live, he said, "in a world
Without heaven to follow." Shall we agree

That we taste heaven only once, when we see
Her at fifteen walking among falling leaves?
It's possible. And yet as Stevens lay dying
He invited the priest in. There, I've said it.

The priest is not an argument, only an instance.
But our gusty emotions say to me that we have
Tasted heaven many times: these delicacies
Are left over from some larger party.

WALLACE STEVENS IN THE FOURTH GRADE

Where a voice that is great within us rises up,
As we stand gazing at the rounded moon.
                    —Wallace Stevens

In the fourth grade he sat on his school bench
Daydreaming. He was already admiring his voice
That he hadn't found. And later on the lawn

He spent hours standing at the edge of Hartford
Looking at the moon. That is where his voice was,
Far up there, in air, near the rounded moon.

He knew the moon was made of clogged magma,
And volcanic rinsings, and punk and dog poop.
That was all right. That was better. It was more

Like us. The rogue moon couldn't hold God
Any longer; we'll have to make do with waltzes,
And Florida and those prancing white horses.

There is no Divine; there are only Viennese horses,
And ordinary evenings and houses. Things have
    changed.
The boy on the bench can become in poems a god.

The Waltz

One man I know keeps saying that we don't need
Heaven. He thinks embroidered Russian
Wedding blouses will take the place of angels;
And windy nights when the crows fly up in front
Of your car will replace all the Psalmists.

He wants us to dance high-hearted, like the bacchae,
Even if it's a waltz. It's a little awkward;
But if you practice, he says, you can do it.
The hard thing is to try to figure out how
To say goodbye—even just going to the grocery.

V

The Neurons Who Watch Birds

We have to think now what it would be like
To be old. Some funny little neurons,
Developed for high-speed runners, and quick-
Handed bowmen, begin to get tired. They fire

But then lay down their bows and watch birds.
The kidney cells—"Too much thinking!" the Chinese
Say—look around for help, but the kids have
All gone to the city. Your friends get hit by lightning,

And your enemies live on. This isn't going to get
Better. Crows yelling from the telephone wires
Don't include you in the stories they tell, and they
    seem
To remember some story that you haven't heard.

What can you do? We'll have to round up
All those little people wandering about
In the body, get them to sit up straight, and study
This problem: How *do* we die?

A Question the Bundle Had

When summer was nearly over,
The bundles would stand in the stubble
Whispering. One said: "For a while,
It looked like I might get away.

"I could have done it—
No one would have noticed.
But it was hard to know
If I should go singly, or with others."

Each of us resembles that
Bundle. For years we waited
For the right moment to escape.
Perhaps it was that moment in July

When the thunder came. But the next
Day it was too late. And we
Ended up in the thresher.
Were we right to wait?

Seeing the Eclipse in Maine

It started about noon. On top of Mount Batte,
We were all exclaiming. Someone had cardboard
And a pin, and we all cried out when the sun
Appeared in tiny form on the notebook cover.

It was hard to believe. The high school teacher
We'd met called it a camera obscura,
People in the Renaissance loved to make them.
Later, when only a sliver was left of the sun,

Light passing through the branches of a fir
Made dozens of crescents all by itself,
Thousands! Even our straw hats produced a few
As we moved them over the bare granite.

We shared chocolate, and one man from Maine
Told a joke. Suns were everywhere at our feet.

CLOTHESPINS

I'd like to have spent my life making
Clothespins. Nothing would be harmed,
Except some pines, probably on land
I owned and would replant. I'd see
My work on clotheslines near some lake,
Up north on a day in October,
Perhaps twelve clothespins, the wood
Still fresh, and a light wind blowing.

The Face in the Toyota

Suppose you see a face in a Toyota
One day, and you fall in love with that face,
And it is Her, and the world rushes by
Like dust blown down a Montana street.

And you fall upward into some deep hole,
And you can't tell God from a grain of sand.
And your life is changed, except that now you
Overlook even more than you did before;

And these ignored things come to bury you,
And you are crushed, and your parents
Can't help anymore, and the woman in the Toyota
Becomes a part of the world that you don't see.

And now the grain of sand becomes sand again,
And you stand on some mountain road weeping.

THE SCANDAL

The day the minister ran off with the choir director
The bindlestiffs felt some gaiety in their arms.
Spike-pitchers threw their bundles higher on the load
And the County Assessor drove with a tiny smile.

Actually the minister's wife felt relieved that
      morning,
Though afraid too. She walked out by the slough,
And admired the beaver's house, partly above
Water, partly beneath. That seemed right.

The minister felt dizzy as the two of them drove
For hours: country music and the loose ribbon
Mingled in his mind with the *Song of Songs*.
They stopped at a small motel near Bismarck.

For the threshers, the stubble was still dry,
The oat dust itchy, the big belt needed grease,
The loads pulled up to the machine. This story
      happens
Over and over, and it's a good story.

Looking at the Stars

I still think about the shepherds, how many stars
They saw. We owe our love of God to these sheep
That had to be followed, or companioned, all night.
One can't just let them run. By midnight

The stars had already become huge talkers.
The Parent sits in her proud Chair, and is punished.
The Dog follows the Hunter. Each time a story ends
There is such a long pause before another begins.

Those of us who are parents, and getting older,
Long, as tonight, for our children to stand
With us, looking at the stars. Here it is,
Eight thousand years later, and I still remember.

AFTER A FRIEND'S DEATH

It must be summer. Push the dock out,
Bring the canoe down, find your old
Books—bird books, Hawthorne. Drive
To Gooseberry. Even in the Swedish islands,

Summer comes. They pull the linen off chairs,
Bring out the blue dishes, write some poems.
Say again: "It must be summer."
Even though people die, it must be summer.

For Orrin

THE PARCEL

It's a parcel of some sort. The exchange
Takes place at night. Sometimes
Dark spots show on the brown wrapping paper,
Because rain was falling.

It happened. The two had met each other only
Yesterday. Neither had read many novels;
They didn't plot this. It had something to do with the
    planets,
With destiny, with rain.

Because it happened, certain gates were shut;
A door opened. Children were born; one died.
How could we call it innocent? The rain
Was innocent.

Do you remember the night of that exchange?
Some forces wanted this to happen.
The rain didn't care, but no one else
Was innocent.

My Doubts on Going to Visit a New Friend

I'm glad that a white horse grazes in that meadow
Outside your kitchen window; even when it rains
There's still someone there. And it rains often
In the mountains.

I have to ask myself what kind of friend I can be.
You'll want to know whether I do dishes,
Or know my share of stories, or any Wallace
Stevens poems by heart.

I know that I won't talk all the time, or steal
Money, or complain about my room,
Or undermine you, or speak disparagingly
Of your family.

I am afraid there'll be a moment when
I fail you, friend; I will turn slightly
Away, our eyes will not meet, and out in the field
There will be no one.

For John

ONE SOURCE OF BAD INFORMATION

There's a boy in you about three
Years old who hasn't learned a thing for thirty
Thousand years. Sometimes it's a girl.

This child had to make up its mind
How to save you from death. He said things like:
"Stay home. Avoid elevators. Eat only elk."

You live with this child, but you don't know it.
You're in the office, yes, but live with this boy
At night. He's uninformed, but he does want

To save your life. And he has. Because of this boy
You survived a lot. He's got six big ideas.
Five don't work. Right now he's repeating them to
　　you.

THOUGHTS

There's something dangerous
In being with good talkers.

The fly's stories of his ancestors
Don't mean much to the frog.

I can't be the noisy person I am
If you don't stop talking.

Some people talk so brilliantly
That we get small and vanish.

The shadows near that Dutch woman
Tell you that Rembrandt is a good listener.

THE GRANDPARENT AND THE GRANDDAUGHTER

"Will you rescue her?" We have dreams like that
When a grandchild is about to be born.
We're called upon and we have to help.
I dreamt that a baby had fallen off a cliff

Into the water. The baby's mouth was opening
And closing. I climbed fast, hand over
Hand down to the shore and pulled her in.
She was all right! That's how I did my part.

The Ocean Rising and Falling

Each fall it rains a lot in the northern woods.
Many parts of our brain hear the rain;
And one part says, "Oh good. Let's sleep."
Another says, "A visitor is coming. It's
A sign!" The oldest brain says: "If that person
Doesn't look like us, we'll stone him." I guess
It's family. The cedar trees mutter,
"About time." Some forest streams
Are amazed to be noticed. Rivers, the big ones, are
    sure
They deserve it. Only the ocean pays no
Attention, being past all that. The ocean just
Goes up and down saying, "I need no more."

OCEAN RAIN AND MUSIC

Rain falls on the shore bushes and the pawky sea
Lettuce, as if it were rain from some other century,
Rain that arrived with the sailing ships,
A steady rain that came out of the Indian ocean
Along with so much music. Well then, since I speak
So affectionately, is it music that has saved me?

Did music become my mother? Music cannot
Close doors, nor keep murderers out.
Some children need to be safe, but most aren't.
Children get born in our world, but who protects
    them?
A few find gypsy wagons and hide there.
The tribe steals them away, and they are gone, for
    now.

I thought to leave with a gypsy troop in my twenties.
Someone did take me away. I had heard
Rumors of heroism. Yeats stole me away.
We leave family and community and never
Get back. But one has to get used to being stolen.
And there are certain secrets that stolen children
    know.

VI

Looking at Aging Faces

Some faces get older and remain who they are. Oh
You can see disappointment there, where parent-
     teacher
Meetings have affected the chin; or the nose got
     pushed
To one side by deaths. So many things happen:
People move away, or your mother becomes crazy
And bites the nurse.

Each face had a long time in the womb to decide
How much it would let worldly things affect it,
How often it would turn toward the wall or the
     woods,
So it didn't have to be seen, how much
It would give in, how stubbornly it would
Hold its own.

Some faces remain whole and radiant. We study them
To find a clue. Aunt Nettie said, "My father
Put on cufflinks every day." Memories like that
Help. One face, as firmly profiled as a hawk,
Used to say: "The world is fair, and if it's not,
I think it is."

For some of us, insults sink in, or the feet
Inherit two roads and lose the way; for others, cold
And hunger come. Some faces change. It's not wrong.
And if you look carefully, you can see,
By glimpsing us just after we wake,
Who we are.

For Bill and Nancy

November

Some aggravations include the whole world.
What can you do? An old pulp-cutter
Longs to die, imagines
The Easter nails.

On his Icelandic farm, Guttorm hears
The news: his two sons
Dead. He pulls the covers
Up over his head.

Some oak leaves hang, others fall.
The body says, "It's all right
To die. It's not an insult
To the world."

Three-Day Fall Rain

The three-day
October rain blows
Leaves down. We knew
That life wouldn't last long.

The dock gleams
With oak leaves, cold
Leaves in the boat, leaves
Spotted in the old man grass.

Hardy warned
Us. Jesus in his boat,
Standing, his back turned,
Being rowed to the other shore.

Winter Afternoon by the Lake

Black trunks, black branches, and white snow.
No one nearby, five o'clock, below zero,
Late January. No birds. No wind.
You look, and your life seems stopped. Perhaps

You died suddenly earlier today. But the thin
Moon says no. The trees say, "It's been this way
Before, often. It's cold, but it's quiet." We've
    experienced
This before, among the messy Saxons putting back

The hide flap. A voice says: "It's old. You'll never
See this again, the way it is now, because
Just today you sensed that someone gave you
Life and said, 'Stay as long as you like.'"

The snow and the black trees, pause, to see if we're
Ready to re-enter that stillness. "Not yet."

For Owen

Isaac Bashevis and Pasternak

Old literary privacies are in danger.
Eudora Welty is eighty, and Hannah Arendt
Is gone. The coelacanth is found more rarely
In the coral off Madagascar. Many of us long

For them. The Kabbalist who sat in Poland,
Eating dry biscuits, the shy painter
Sleeping in his studio, watching the light, in love
With green and orange, who has replaced them?

Is a flavor, once in the water, a gift from fallen
Oak leaves, gone? This water stained with old
Privacies that once stood in barrels from Sicily
To Norway—tell me where I can find it.

People Like Us

There are more like us. All over the world
There are confused people, who can't remember
The name of their dog when they wake up, and
    people
Who love God but can't remember where

He was when they went to sleep. It's
All right. The world cleanses itself this way.
A wrong number occurs to you in the middle
Of the night, you dial it, it rings just in time

To save the house. And the second-story man
Gets the wrong address, where the insomniac lives,
And he's lonely, and they talk, and the thief
Goes back to college. Even in graduate school,

You can wander into the wrong classroom,
And hear great poems lovingly spoken
By the wrong professor. And you find your soul,
And greatness has a defender, and even in death
    you're safe.

For James Wright

A Christmas Poem

Christmas is a place, like Jackson Hole, where we all
    agree
To meet once a year. It has water, and grass for
    horses;
All the fur traders can come in. We visited the place
As children, but we never heard the good stories.

Those stories only get told in the big tents, late
At night, when a trapper who has been caught
In his own trap, held down in icy water, talks; and a
    man
With a ponytail and a limp comes in from the edge of
    the fire.

As children, we knew there was more to it—
Why some men got drunk on Christmas Eve
Wasn't explained, nor why we were so often
Near tears nor why the stars came down so close,

Why so much was lost. Those men and women
Who had died in wars started by others,
Did they come that night? Is that why the Christmas
    tree
Trembled just before we opened the presents?

There was something about angels. *Angels we*
Have heard on high Sweetly singing o'er
The plain. The angels were certain. But we could not
Be certain whether our family was worthy tonight.

READING *SILENCE IN THE SNOWY FIELDS*

A word I love comes—snow; then fencepost
And dust and grass and night and barndoor,
Also light pole and cottonwood, but seldom *you*.
That's how the words flowed when I was thirty,

Or even forty. It's as if some furtive men said,
"This word *you* is not right. It would lead you
To imagine closeness. We know that
Won't happen. We have your best interests in mind."

The bitter ones—the old ones—lived
Inside the Shirley Temple creamers of blue glass
That stood on our kitchen table; they blessed us,
We thought, along with the County Extension Agent,

The movies, and the *Philip Morris Mystery Theater.*
Some mornings I close my ears to these voices—
I abandon all the blue glass in the world to them—
Then I too speak this beautiful word *you*.

Words the Dreamer Spoke to My Father in Maine

Ocean light as we wake reminds us how dark
Our old house is. That's home. Like Hamlet,
One visit to Wittenberg is enough, and we'll soon be
Back in crazy Denmark. I dreamt I stood

In a machine shop; my dead father stands beside me.
We talk, but his eyes remain on my chest.
I say to him for the first time: "Oh look at me
When we talk." I could see cubbyholes

With dark tools, and a rough floor stained with oil.
Clotted windows, cobwebs, a black vise.
But sunlight outside our windows speaks of ocean
Light, bone light, Labrador light, prairie light.

It's the same light that glints off swords, and shines
From Idaho rivers some days, and from the thin
Face just before death. I say to my father,
"We could be there if we could lift our eyes."

Visiting Sand Island

Somebody showed off and tried to tell the truth
And drank wine and went to bed. Someone
Woke in the night and wanted his children
To walk in the grass on this island under the stars.

Someone was lucky. Someone had eyes and found
Stars. Someone had feet and found grass.
Someone loved thought, and knew things to learn.
Someone could turn in the river and go up or down.

Someone thought he was unlucky, thought he didn't
    try
To tell the truth. Someone thought his head was dark.
Someone tried to feel as bad as others did; someone
Flapped along the ground to draw the fox to him.

Tell him, friends, that the nest is now gone;
Tell him the little twigs are all dispersed.
Tell him all he has to do is walk under stars.
Tell him the fox has long since eaten his dinner.

A Poem for Giambattista Vico Written by the Pacific

A rephrasing of Vico:
All cultures go through three stages. Culture moves from the
Sacred World to the Aristocratic Realm to the Democratic
Place, and back again.

I.

We were sitting there, badly blessed, and brooding
On aristocracies near the trouserless ocean.
We knew we were pure prose; the ocean stretched
Out, blown by wind, but we remained where we
    were.
The sand shifted; all of us walked on flat boards.
We were no one in particular, in our messy lives.
We tended to stay who we were. Our minds stay in
    this
Particular room with Nils and Judy and Tom.
If death is the mother of fashion, we don't mind.
I am myself; I am what is around me.
Pine cones fall and stick where they fall.
That is what it's like when we are born
Not from wind or spirit, but from things.

2.

Spirit moves where it moves; that is what
People are like who are born of the Spirit.
For in high air there burns a furious spirit.
It rises out of ground like Milton's mind
That meets all furies high above the sea.
It wants to rise. "If music be the food of love,
Play on." So notes, inspired not by our toes
But by th'inspired intellect, take us
Out of the dark soul-house, upward through turns
And spiral stairs, fighting the darken'd air.
The Spirit carries us, and in our minds
We know if we are high or not. It is
Something like this for those still in the Spirit.

3.

The wind blows where it likes: that is what
Everyone is like who is born from the wind.
Oh now it's getting serious. We want to be those
Born from the wind that blows along the plains
And over the sea where no one has a home.
And that Upsetting Rabbi, didn't he say:
"Take nothing with you, no blanket, no bread.
When evening comes, sleep wherever you are.

And if the owners say no, shake out the dust
From your sandals; leave the dust on their doorstep."
Don't hope for what will never come. Give up hope,
Dear friends, the joists of life are laid on the winds.

FOR RUTH

There's a graceful way of doing things. Birch
    branches
Curve slightly upward; or the wind brings a few
Snowflakes down, and then joins the night;
Or you leave me a sprig of chervil and no more.

Each morning we have this new chance. We can walk
A few steps behind the others down the mountain;
We can enter a conversation as if we were blessed,
Not insisting on our old way of gaining pity.

There's a way you have of knowing what another
May need ahead of time, before the party
Begins, as smoke sometimes disappears
Downward among branches. And I've learned

From you this new way of letting a poem be.

A Conversation with a Mouse

One day a mouse called to me from his curly nest:
"How do you sleep? I love curliness."

"Well, I like to be stretched out. I like my bones to be
All lined up. I like to see my toes way off over there."

"I suppose that's one way," the mouse said, "but I
    don't like it.
The planets don't act that way, nor the Milky Way."

What could I say? You know you're near the end
Of the century when a sleepy mouse brings in the
    Milky Way.